ETERNAL ICONS

ETERNAL ICONS

IVY BLAIR

CONTENTS

1 Introduction   1

2 Defining Icons   3

3 Historical Icons   7

4 Modern Icons   11

5 Cultural Impact   15

6 Artistic Legacy   19

7 Innovators and Trailblazers   23

8 Icons of Compassion   27

9 Icons of Entertainment   31

10 Musical Legends   35

11 Fashion and Style Icons   39

12 Sports Icons   43

13 Enduring Influence   45

14 Conclusion   47

CHAPTER 1

Introduction

Welcome to Eternal Icons: Life and Legacy in Popular Culture. This is the opening chapter of the book. In Page-Turners, Sayers and Gould present a work aimed at anyone who has a fascination with larger-than-life figures, who intrinsically understand what makes an individual or a team of people successful in the public sphere. We address celebrity, stardom, and iconic status as loci of rebelliousness against social conventions, stereotypes, and taboos. To begin, stardom has long been recognized as presenting the ideal forum for living with pizzazz. The twenty-first century has worshipped at the twin gods of celebrity and stardom in unprecedented numbers. The glossy magazine now sells far more copies than the tabloid, and TV audiences of all ages tune into specific shows, monthly specials, one-off documentaries, and the continuous line of chat shows dominated on both sides of the Atlantic by hosts whose interview style has been honed to mirror the excesses of the modern era. This is not trivial gossip; our unparalleled fascination feeds news media and webs, leading to a greater public profile. There are desired outcomes in this modern memory. Cary Cooper and Mark Hampton ask how living iconoclasts face these challenges in this electric haze?

You Are Family Comprising eleven chapters, Furthermore and Frith explore the changing face of celebrity, the co-production of a plethora of hero-like characters, and the disneyfication of old legends and myths. The idols we examine come from ABC and EST family values of the planet's pre-eminent superpower. They fill mega-stadia around the globe. As cultural entrepreneur Terry Allen remarks, these music idols perpetuate each other. Their influence penetrates design, catwalks, food, and fashion of global all-sorts and informed discourse, yet hedging urban and rural consumption of low-culture artifacts that critics love to hate. They are folkloric authorities and express public sensibilities who've influenced performance, origin narrative, mega concert, and contemporary aspiration. These eternal icons tend to transcend their death, of which there are at least three layers to consider. In US popular culture, a figure like John Wayne serves to highlight key influence over birth, life, and death. The act of dying might hold constant, but response varies. The new revival is to hold multiple memorial services: one at the time of death, and the next at a later date.

CHAPTER 2

Defining Icons

The concept of an 'icon' extends beyond being a generally familiar vocabulary word; its definition, often accompanied by superlatives such as 'living legend', 'groundbreaking', 'pioneering' and 'torchbearer', is cogent enough that it necessitates no dictionary referral. But what, indeed, raises someone above superstardom? Which department do icons head, and what documents or tools do they use when they attempt to inflate their followers? This section attempts to grasp the complexities of iconic attributes, aspiring to capture criteria that might be employed to categorize and quantify varying shades and gradients within those characteristics.

Oft rather too warily conflated with figures admired simply for their general star appeal, 'celebrity' and 'icon' have distinct denotations; whereas celebrities are individuals primarily acclaimed for their recognizability, association with contested 'talents' and fortune of personality-based renown, icons are players of more rarified games, commended for having produced in their respective fields work of a particular standard of innovation, discipline and durability. Outshining reputations that strike favour with a 'time of the casting' flourish and ebb, 'icon' is an accolade earned by those who outpace these bandwagons to ride piggyback upon diffusion channels named half-forgotten eras, indomitably extending themselves as role models - cultural emblems - whose influence envelops not only art, indeed, but politics, technology, sexual mores and other facets of 'real life'. Observed in the flesh and blood these are the ones who will outlast their fellow 'reality heyday' luminaries as aspirational archetype of a distinct practice.

Although many qualities make an 'icon' (Katharina Stenske argues a sort of "white knight/Joan-of-Arc" resonance), the baseline description of one may well be "a mimeograph of some antique, shared wisdom gleaned from Verdi or Cleopatra, Oprah or Marc Terenzi". As an expression extending beyond the items of affection offered rulers, and a priorite borner than either a 'cult figure' or 'role model', an icon is a taken-for-granted standard of near-universal standard of behaviour, recognition, anti-rejection or respect. The same term, when employed in Internet usage, typically refers to super-hi-res, Windows xp-friendly .ico files which float around Web dev community, providing a pixellated likeness of (but not a substitute for) various products which are as yet to even penetrate or endeavour to "fend for one's self" in the market some might term "somark".

What Makes a Celebrity an Icon

Many celebrities are loved and admired, but some stand out to become icons – celebrities who are often seen as some of the greatest in history. These are the people who set trends, change lives, and become larger than life. Some of these celebrities might not have been popular during their time, but everything changed after their death – like in the case of Vincent Van Gogh, who is appreciated as a genius today despite not achieving any success during his lifetime. An iconic celebrity is a powerful presence that unites our culture and crosses generations. Some celebrities are here today, gone tomorrow. But a celebrity becoming an icon is forever.

What makes someone go from being an ordinary celebrity to becoming an icon? Somebody becomes an icon because we have decided that the person or character is symbolic of something – something intertwined with the world. Usually, this can be summed up in a single word – like 'iconic', of course. But the ripple effect continues. Even if it is forgotten, we have made an indexical link to Brigitte Bardot's provocation, Charlize Theron's transformation, or even the Pierce Brosnan hat-tilt. When we think of a certain word or phenomenon, we think of a timeless association with an association from a very specific time or place. Disney's ever-expanding array of movies or the occasional movie-set luxury handbag has set likes and dislikes on each of these fashion trends. Celebrity is their most obvious and most lucrative target. Whether we like the celebrities associated with these worlds or not, they have entered the stratosphere of coolness where any negative reaction is in celebration of a known cliché.

CHAPTER 3

Historical Icons

What makes an icon? Certainly, there are large numbers of individuals who have achieved some degree of celebrity but have not withstood the test of time. Their fame is destined to be extinguished one day. The twenty-first century has already seen its share of beloved actors, musicians, and television personalities pass away. Some are young, some old. Some die peacefully, while others suffer from a mental health crisis. Those who survive and thrive in this area to the present day tend to be forgotten. With the passage of time, literacy can be provided to a few selected individuals who were noteworthy. These important figures were renowned in ancient times and their renown has only grown over time. Their outstanding achievements, kind characters, and dramatic lives have given them a great reputation. Many erudites have delved into their lives and family histories. They are both free to adopt and to greet. What's in store is, obviously, the small matter of historical personality and the extent of the documentary evidence that has been overlooked.

Claudius Caesar was a Roman emperor who ruled Rome in AD 54–68. In his late forties, he had a stammer and a limp, and he was thought to be a fool. Even today, his nickname, "old clod," has a tendency to draw us in. Or deified Augustus, a leathered character to whom we have already dedicated the first lesson of the spring quarter: March 31, 2017. A man of many triumphs, including the establishment of the principate and the end of the Roman Republic. We stare quietly at that calm, unmoved statue and explore the many secrets of the state hidden within. (This is, of necessity, before receiving a thorough check to confirm!) From the Consulate of the Empire to the epic invasion of Britannia, we are gripped by the man-made history event.

Ancient Icons

Icons are the most influential and beloved people in their field, making long-lasting impacts in not only their industry, but history as well. These are the individuals considered to be legends of all time and people who remain a recognizable name with lasting legacies. This list ranges from politicians to dynasties to military leaders and beyond. Icons may be revered, hated, or simply recognized. This article will be devoted to ancient icons. These are: King Tutankhamun, Cleopatra, Gilgamesh, Ramses II, Nefertiti, Cyrus the Great, Alexander the Great, Julius Caesar.

Tutankhamun lived from around 1340 B.C.E until 1323 B.C.E. His father, Pharaoh Akhenaten, moved the capital of the Egyptian empire to Amarna and crushed traditional religious beliefs to make Aten, the sun, the only recognized god. As a result of his father's actions, Egypt lost some international prestige. At age nine, Tutankhamun was crowned pharaoh of Egypt. About six years later, he died suddenly. According to DNA testing, he died of an inherited disorder called Kohler's disease that weakened his bones and led to death. Despite his young age, King Tutankhamun is one of the most famous ancient icons in Egyptian history. The pharaoh is best known for "King Tut's" tomb, which was discovered in 1922 by British archaeologist Howard Carter.

Innermost of four nested coffins of Tutankhamun. Memoirs of the Metropolitan Museum of Art 50; 58, 201-217 Smekare with Tutankhamun and Ay. He came to the throne when he was nine, and it is assumed that he died when he was about 18 or 19. Only about 20 when he died, he is one of the best-known of Ancient Egypt's 170 or more pharaohs and cannot be said to be one of the greatest. There was frustration and turmoil in Ancient Egypt during Tutankhamun's reign. In the fourth year of his reign, high officials began to plot against him, endangering the dynasty's survival. They were not able to carry out their plans. There is a relief carving of the assassination of Tutankhamun on the wall of the tomb of one of the high officials, Ramosef of Heliopolis.

CHAPTER 4

Modern Icons

Critics have long suggested that we have recently witnessed the birth of new iconic figures. This view raises a number of questions about the nature and function of icons. We need to know what these new icons have achieved and the qualities that such a title involves. Are these millions-strong idols genuinely worthy of great public respect? We must also ask ourselves how our brand of icon affects our own lives and the nature of the world we live in. At the same time, we must question why critics such as Pipi Weise, who told Twilight Saga star Kristen Stewart in a lengthy insightful Sunday Times article in 2010, that "you belong to the age that you live in," firmly believe that printed magazines still have the power to continue this tradition of fame-making.

To the critically-minded, icons are usually dead. Throughout history, well-loved individuals synonymous with genuine admiration from millions have passed and continue to live through paintings, illustrated writings, screenplays, and beloved stories. Recipients of this accolade often have grounded principles or talents and have become so known for their "real person" label, like the subject or object of folklore and tall tales. Given all of this, we may ask ourselves what makes our contemporaries different and so uniquely iconic that their mystical untouchable qualities are continuing to rise.

20th Century Icons

The 20th century saw the rise of a new type of icon: the celebrity. The century was the birth of cinema, meaning performers and actresses could reach an audience like never before, and it is the start of the music industry with vinyl pressed records are able to be played in the home. Icons throughout the century played with the concept of the "alluring wretchedness, poets of heavenly ideals and bottomless depths, bastions of beautifying horror, mariners upon the boundless ebb and flow of the moods of a rebellious and decreating chthonian and overhanging all". An artist of this time was given the charge of being both human and humankind, always in front of the blazing of the Dionysian light. The artist is also charged to reveal the platonic in the most base of actions.

To be comfortable in one's flesh seems to go against the definition, at least according to some. At the end of the day, to be Dionysian is to be slippery. Arguably, Marilyn Monroe was Dionysian. There might have been few in the 20th century who captured the attention of the world. Rock and roll philosopher Terence McKenna thought in case of nuclear holocaust one might go "at least I lived when Marilyn Monroe lived". Whatever Monroe had was electric, magnetizing the people she met and the world at large. Apologist and Antagonist alike can argue that Monroe was much more than what she seemed: a dedicated reader of Joyce, a follower of Beat poetry, a devoted friend of Frank Sinatra and Salvador Dali. Physicists of time the world over muse on the subject during lectures. Would earth move as fast to the present without a Monroe? Speculation might be futile. What cannot be disputed is how much and how lasting Monroe's image has been. Dress fluttering in the breeze standing on hot air vent – without a face, it is Monroe. Oscillating on a jack-in-the-box to the sound of Happy Birthday, instantly orating the JFK birthday song. A battered life that was once a little orb-shaped thing now arguably equals JFK - a US president in Welsh. Monroe, the part of her that is etched in the collective memory of many, is a complex weave of image and phantasm that she may never fully realize nor appreciate. Perhaps Monroe was an icon regardless of herself. She was the tray of dress, makeup, and jewels. To some, she was also the lady of sorrow, probably not knowingly whistled haunted, bluesy, jazz notes at a similar time the term ghoul was being used as a label. Whatever Marilyn was, the label endures. Long after her death, it was the first conversation overheard: "Who are the icons of the era?". It may just be that iconic status is never certain in the present. Every once in a while, someone may hit the target.

CHAPTER 5

Cultural Impact

Along with an immeasurable cultural impact, these venerated personalities manage to touch various corners of the earth and transcend time itself. Timeless celebrities shape entire segments of numerous society's values, stances, and beliefs. The detailed reasons for these types of adorations are frequently intricately individual and specific to the experience of a cultural group. Beyond these idiosyncrasies, however, we are frequently also imbued with a sense of the universal - the understanding that our connection to these figures resonates with others far removed from us by place or time. That sense of the universal does more than build communities of admirers. It also provides the basis for a 'what-if' game that spans time and space. This game asks a simple question that provides a multitude of answers and tells a storied history of the world and the people within it.

As we take stock of our living heroes and icons, who makes the list? Just as importantly, what connects these icons across time and space? Scholars have suggested different selection criteria for eternal icons. Some believe in the idea of a 'universal' audience - an intangible metric against which we measure a personality's global popularity. For others, an icon presents a certain ambiguity that makes his or her meaning translatable to different cultures, even while offering a particular reading to locals familiar with the idol's work. Hosts of museums, for instance, have celebrated the Indian film star Amitabh Bachchan and Mexican ranchera singer, Pedro Infante, who died ages ago but continue to sustain powerful and embracing presences in the lives of fans, youthful and aged, around the world.

Icons Across Different Cultures

It would be a mistake to call an icon a worldwide celebrity, yet the meaning of an eternal uniting figure across different nationalities is close to it. In addition, noble and exquisite, icons strike with their divinity. Be it a 'she' or a 'he', one thing is certain – an icon as a universally adored public figure also transcends national borders, albeit due to entirely different reasons compared to brands and perhaps in a more critical manner than brands. An eternal icon is a universally admired and most frequently emulated or identified with celebrity and it does not have to be famous for the masses in order to achieve that. For a more localized populace – an idol can still be the best football player of the country, a silver medal-winning national ice-skater, a humanitarian worker with decades of selfless dedication or an established and prestigious war artist.

Iconography shares in common more narratives of individual tendencies – the new definition emphasizes personal and experiential identification with a leader. Timeless icons have been recognized as guiding figures in areas well beyond advertising – fashion, films and other entertainment, sports, social media – with a dedicating public that spans any nationality, cultural background, age, sex and other demographic factors. In a more philosophical or sociological context, the paths of icons and the paradigms of individualism can also be cross-connected. It is also critical to understand the cultural capital that successful branding has garnered for a new line of product or service. Thus, whether an individual person is an eternal icon or an immortal image, having an individual and personal identity or grammar attached to a brand can undoubtedly indicate a successful outcome of a branding business venture.

CHAPTER 6

Artistic Legacy

Since the early seventies of the 20th century, the concept of celebrities has become quite wide and now applies not only to the world of show business. Originally, the term 'celebrity' meant a famous person, or one who is well known within a system of power structure. At present, the concept has become so established that it refers to all people widely known and popular in society. Not met at all in newspapers, world classics in literature - the second self most eulogy/obituary wherein hopelessly mixed fifteen different Leitmotif: a spurious, syncretic array of status reports. Tenor celebrity literature occupies justifiable the authors of the standard gang of the immutable. Accordingly, celebrities in literature reflect the spirit of their generation (wants and needs) although surpassed also that era. Icons remain silent: ever since they are blowing. Artistic memory is called the most long-lived and dry of all.

With reference to these features of timeless celebrities, we suggest a brief revue of artistic representation in their case. For centuries, artists have been inspired by celebrated persons and have found visual ways to recognize those individuals who have had the greatest impact on society in their time or who, in their opinion, would qualitatively alter the human spirit and physical constitution by the art or the ability exuded. This cultural veneration of those considered as 'icons' or persons with 'magnetism' has occurred from the remote past to the present. Throughout history, a large array of media has become a vehicle for such emulation and, paradoxically or not, seen the likes of iconic person-inspired merchandise dotted around art shops and museums, including postcards and posters. Whether through visual arts or literature, these icons were meant to be known within the confines of popularity and tradition of our fathers. In a very real sense, Janson points out that a celebrity is the selection of society. Such figures also tended to elicit passionate reactions of hatred along with love, as the gulf between the high ground and the lowly path was crossed through the universal human capability and perhaps 'sophistication'. From a chronological spectrum, iconic figures have arisen with the continuation of 'written' history - as legends in the Pharaonic age, immortalized in the Rosetta Stone; Jesus of Nazareth with various representations from early Coptic to female, and Krishna appearing in human guise upheld Krishna's charm as expounded in the Bible. With the rise of industrialization in the world, celebrities gradually became more and more an offshoot of individuals 'produced' by an age that was slowly phasing in the electronic age.

Icons in Art and Literature

In the domains of art and literature, authors and artists alike have been inspired by the charisma, charm, and emotional ethos exuded by an icon such as Diana or Marilyn. Although the icons may have met a premature and tragic death, their abiding attraction and the magnetic hold they continue to exert on their fans seem to have nurtured and encouraged numerous artists, including some of the world's greatest communicators and craftspeople. Fyfe opines: 'Call them pictorial masterpieces or multilingual masterpieces; the art Master who meets them in the National Gallery or the artist-critic who meets them on his way to his study...' In literature, the iconic personalities have similarly become fictional as well as poetic characters, lending themselves to a powerful theme or motif.

Ross King, in Leonardo and The Last Supper, claims that conspicuous autographs in a painting, which should neither withhold nor obtrude itself, link artistic with iconic appreciation. Yet although the portrait may stress the personality of the sitter, in art, an apparently straightforward representation of a single identity can acquire an altogether different, multifarious, literary, and iconic/hermeneutical significance, capable of illustration and encouragement for every viewer. As a consequence, the 'icon of Marilyn' thus becomes more than the face of the dead American star: she becomes, as Campbell has proclaimed, one 'symbol of woman' that has shown the 'face and transfiguration of soul'. Like the Mona Lisa, throughout art history, other such fashionable feminine archetypes of iconic semblance, assuming configurations of endless eloquence and self-deifying brio, have served as artistic inspiration. Queen Elizabeth I, the Empress Josephine, and the Duchess of Castiglione stand out as popular artistic 'muses' of regnant bearing. In this cinematic aspect, too, the icon emerges as a composite character 'a blend of different roles and cultural references'. In literature and art, icons, broadly speaking, have been celebrated as heroes and become personae of high sensual allure.

CHAPTER 7

Innovators and Trailblazers

Throughout history, there have been many people who have made a difference in their respective fields of expertise, but only the most deserving of these individuals remain forever in the hearts of, and continue to make a difference in the lives of, the people they have touched. Innovators and trailblazers from the extraordinary world of technology are always remembered for their brilliant ideas and perseverance in the world of science and technology. Many men have carved a niche in the world of technology, made an impact and become a household name. Yet others achieved so much more and become a brand name. They transformed the world of technology and became synonymous with innovation and technology itself. Their ideas, thought and imagination still remains the backbone of modern technology. As we look back at them, we remember them as unlimited innovators and eternal celebrities of this world. It is just because of these celebrities, we speak of such a brilliant technology that world itself laughs.

This list of extraordinary tech figures includes many who pose a challenge to the respected celebrities, from the realm of technology and made monumental developments in their realms. It is always the less obvious breakthrough, or a serial line of developments, that leaves a mark in scientific history; those who developed the prototype or laid the foundations. Such brilliant minds, who master the resources at their disposal only to bring in further progress, ushering in a new era, are our chosen celebrities who built the platforms for the future; those who willow the future generations with a proud, resolute, maverick heritage. To achieve such hydrantrcy, celebrities are talented innovators who with their research and developments, have laid down the cornerstones of modern technology. The most influential figures, when it comes to the worlds of science and technology, have never made the Forbes "Top 50 richest men in the world" list—or Krishna (or Kerry) list, or Gates list, for that matter. They have been, and continue to be, the legend and pride of the world today.

Icons in Science and Technology

Historically, the stories of science and technology often present us with a 'standard model' of great men: geniuses and visionaries whose ideas and aspirations have shaped the technological world in their own image. In reality, these iconic celebrities of science and technology have often been supported, sometimes unwittingly, by a cast of thousands of less famous actors: shop workers, industrialists, foremen, labourers, craftspersons, gardeners, and others. The well-worn 'footnote' cliche about 'giants standing on the shoulders of little people' belies the fact that the 'little people' were often giants in their own right. We aim to highlight the achievements of these one-time giants encapsulated in a burgeoning contemporary scholarship, symbolized by conferences, collections of academic papers, even a new journal called the ICON journal.

In this essay, we present portraits of seven icons of science and technology. Their stories suggest the potential in the icon concept, because they are concretized in the places wherein they worked, as well as artifacts and practices they helped to transform. We will discuss the Harry Stevinson air-powered bicycle that led to the $6,000 Glidden 'Prize' in the fall of 1976 won by a 'Canadian 'flying winnebago,' the AvroVancraft, ridden by Fred Rompell and Tom Parizo. Stevinson was a can-do engineer at heart and a 'blacksmith' (welder) by trade. Together with his astute talent for poultry farming, he made numerous contributions to Avro: high-speed structural welding of jet aircraft, nuclear aircraft, road building machines, the Avro car, and a high-speed hovercraft. Justification received.

CHAPTER 8

Icons of Compassion

Amidst the darkness of the world, there are those who shine their light in an effort to make things brighter for the future. Some of those have made enough of an impact to be celebrated as icons of compassion. Addressing a litany of important world issues through various philanthropic means, these icons have shown the world that true success is measured by how much good one does for another. There is no limit to how pure and compassionate one can be, no standard to giving, and no height to how sophisticated humanity can mature to be – these are the guiding truths that an icon of compassion radiates from every action they take, and every word they speak. These living saints have explored the charitable fabric of humanity, and proven, unequivocally, that compassion and forthrightness elevate us from the human standpoint to the humane ideal.

By their selfless acts of generosity and countless hours of dedicated work, these icons of compassion are making an everlasting impression in our world, and while they may not seek any form of honor for the life-saving work they do, we at Eternal Icons celebrate them. We believe that they serve as an example, teaching us that it is not what we accumulate that matters most, but what we do with what we have. Their lives remind us that we are only so rich as we share what we have; only so enlightened as we look beyond ourselves, only so important as we are to those who are less fortunate, and only so remembered as we can reach out and touch a life with our hearts. Later in this book, we will detail 100 charities that represent part of the legacy of caring that our icons of compassion are remembered for, as well as the champions around our world who carry forward this work today. These selected few icons are a further representative sample of the multitude of individuals and charities who share such an unselfish nature. We at Eternal Icons are honored to represent them as part of our Lifetime Achievement Series.

Humanitarian Icons

Humanitarian The Vietnam War was one of the darkest war episodes in the history of the United States. Many symbols of the American way of life were challenged, but perhaps none more than this little girl: Phan Thi Kim Phuc. After a napalm attack in 1972, Phan ran down the road, screaming in agony and horror as colorful flames consumed her neighborhood and family. Photographer Nick Ut captured the infamous napalm girl photo. That one photo became a powerful moment between enemies fighting in Vietnam and eventually the United States Congress. It testified to the horrors of war and the full extent of medicine to help all humanity. Phan was a living symbol of the eternal victims of war, but she has found a very different purpose in life since the end of the war.

For more than 20 years, Kim Phuc has been actively involved in humanitarian work to help children of war. Since the birth of Kim Foundation for Child Eradication of War in 1997, she has been highly regarded around the world by children, advocates, and supporters of permanent norms. Goodwill colleagues included the likes of Kim UN Goodwill, Mr. Gorny Stant, UN Secretary-General Annan. Kim and the Board of Directors are also invited to the UN

General Assembly to vote on normal permanent projects and in the future as a formal representative of the international community's permanent time. They are especially committed to the important political issue of the UN, for the long term and for the coming generations. To protect the future children of the war, Kim has promoted collaboration with the United Nations and its representatives. In particular, for more than a decade, she has helped collect and tell the stories from organizations that link hands of shoes between small actions and major changes. She has personally visited and promoted, especially, the permanent solutions aimed at sharing, rehabilitating, and saving the children in war between the present and the next generation. She was giving ordinary people a chance to help save the future of the planet. Kim's work has been recognized and honored by the international community, billions of children, and governments around the world. She has spoken at the United Nations and, as part of a Nobel Peace Prize-winning crisis conference together with 4 other good-faith will, has pledged ethical obligations to find a permanent solution to a global crisis which affects 300,000 children in region 53 in more than 60 years, mostly in developing countries.

CHAPTER 9

Icons of Entertainment

Since the earliest days of modern entertainment, the silver screen revolutionized the way people all over the world consume information. Some actors, musicians, and public figures have made lasting impacts on the industry and the general public, who saw them as larger than life. Beloved celebrities of this sort have been immortalized either within a specific franchise or in film entertainment in general. When they pass away, their names and roles will continue to be spoken of as long as their films are being watched, often remade, and even sometimes surpassed. With the coining of the term 'blockbuster' in the late 1970s, stars who were able to captivate audiences with their on-screen presence alone became true movie icons, and their passing brought upon a period of collective remembrance, praise, and contemplation, such as John Wayne (d. 1979), James Stewart (d. 1997), Gene Kelly (d. 1996), and Marilyn Monroe (d. 1962).

People of a more recent generation have never known a time without television or computers. The past two decades with the increase of easy access technology has had massive changes. The celebrities who have passed away during this recent period are just now starting to discover the hold that these celebrities had on everyday life. Silent movie stars Douglas Fairbanks, Al Jolson, and Harry

Houdini made lasting impacts upon society. After the adoption phenomenon of MTV in the 1980s, major music stars or music personalities from the past have been taken from us. Some of the deceased include Kurt Cobain, Michael Jackson, Whitney Houston, Aaliyah, Notorious B.I.G., and Tupac Shakur. Newly deceased celebrities have been from a more diverse crowd: sportscaster John Madden, model Anna Nicole Smith, actor Burt Reynolds, and wrestler Owen Hart. Each of these figures held small parts in our lives that few of us would ever forget.

Film and Television Icons

Regardless of the industry, the word "icon" holds a similar connotation, evoking the image of a paragon or a celebrated figurehead. In the world of film and television, icons regularly arise and etch a lasting impact upon their industry. But what is an icon? An icon is a symbol of historical, cultural, or emotional significance; it is a singular figure or work with an astral resonance. They are the stories of the first vampire, the seven samurai, the overextended Roman Empire, and the 22nd Maine Infantry. They are windows into the realm of myth that reveal something beautiful and moving about humanity. Consequently, it should come as no surprise that characters and performers who claim the title of "icon" share a special affinity with the Academy, already known for venerating history.

There is also a sense in which icons, being both familiar and exceptional, also capture a quintessential aspect of the ecstatic, the demure. They are at once grounded and transcendent, a weave of the resonant and the disorienting. To watch an icon on screen is to overperceive each movement, as a crowd at a historical event or sinner at the station of a saint. They infuse preposterous plots with heart-stuttering tension; they fire awkward or patently absurd dialogue from the riffle of recitation into the hail of divine improvisation. A mediocre film becomes a "star vehicle," with the icon's light and personality taking precedence over little narrative bits; a solid screenplay is made transcendent, through deconstruction. Usually, an actor or characters reach for the icon when they slow down, hold back from the fray. They mime, humorously, the garlands and incense of the process, in overtly humbling notions of inspiration and friendship. Because to put oneself in the pantheon of pouting Garbos while still moving furniture around in a way only a mortal can is social vaudeville, and our empathy.

Other would-be icons find themselves bore out of, and seem ultimately less luminous than, their context and the controversy they inspired. Hussey revivified Oscar Wilde in 1968's The Roman Spring of Mrs. Stone, a borderline appropriate, toe-curlingly forgotten gem for those looking to relive Merchant Ivory balled up into a toffee; she also was "extra" enough to appear in one of the worst-ever Masterpiece Theaters, the 1977 Les Miserables adaptation as default dolly Cosette, whom Sue Johnston then knocked dead in the 1997 pick up episode of Goggle Eyes. Mary Tyler Moore wasn't exactly blow cord like Jayne Mansfield in the body department, but she was game enough on The Mary Tyler Moore Show that enough of her other characters, be they housewives in veils or elderly in veils or advice columnist local hate acquisition manager in veils, could endear in sufficient volume for us to tech translator HDTV onto a loving porpoise that to "having a little strep situation." All due respect to Dame Angela: the people are in no rush to swallow spun-on Ethel.

CHAPTER 10

Musical Legends

Few and far between are the musical legends, unbelievably talented artists who come but once in a century. However different they may be from each other, be it in their music influences or in their public persona, the contemporaries argue that their extraordinary gift is what gives life to their music. Every time they release a piece, it feels just as fresh. It transports the listener to a unique place with each listen, so human, so transcendent at once. These acts like Nina Simone, Duke Ellington, Jimi Hendrix, Stevie Wonder, John Coltrane, Édith Piaf, Nat King Cole, Jeff Buckley, and Freddie Mercury all had legendary careers. Not only did they all have a major impact on the music industry, but they also changed music forever.

Their music is something that will most likely never be repeated. Duke Ellington, smooth as sherry, hard as oak, plays music to enthrall the air over and over again; Nat "Oh La La" Cole remains one of the very greatest entertainers anywhere, Stevie Wonder is a wizard on the harmonica. The Quicksilver Jackson has a great voice and a lot of jazz for any kind of pianist—he's a soul stylist with a great technique, John Coltrane and the convulsionist quartet spread fire and swing, with amazing sibilations and an obstreperous tenor. From then on, from Nina on, it's another planet, that of the very highest achievement in jazz, as it is played and sung. Jimi Hendrix has become a vulture cry echoing across the sky, eccentrically wealthy and comfortably alive. Nina Simone's piano brings back the importance of singing the blues in jazz, while another singer-pianist who doesn't make records, "the CAT", Mary Lou Williams, explodes with creativity. Jimi Hendrix lives in the Now and projects a fireball tomorrow.

Icons in the Music Industry

An icon is an individual who has become emblematic of their chosen field. An icon holds not just an affirming place in the annals of their particular line of work, but tends to serve as a cultural touchstone for entire swathes of civilization. In the context of music, entire genres have been launched off of the success of an iconic band or song as audiences become captivated by what can be achieved in this particular vein. It is easy to see why icons are so deeply celebrated and keenly studied, and so it is also understandable as to why new icons seem to break on the shore of public conscience with tantalizing infrequency. These are not simply celebrities, although that is self-evidently a part of their story, but larger-than-life presences whose influence is only truly felt in the weeks and years subsequent to their passing. That is to say, according to the prevailing belief and diction of this discourse, that icons are those-in-the-know who have caught the world's attention at some point during their lives and never really let go.

Music, as it branches into so many disparate and populous sub-threads, is an especially fertile ground for producing the rare and rewarding stripe of individual. Any number of bardic luminaries from throughout history's pages are celebrated figures all of the way into the modern day. A relative few of these same sages are viewed as common-sense personalities whose features and subtler attributes can be brought forward with only a slight scratch or a smidgen of dust steaming off of a rug. This piece is dedicated to what we might call icons as they're often celebrated and most often understood, and as such are beloved for their performances and the people that they become over the course of their globetrotting lives. The space afforded here is hardly enough to ably catalogue all of these important figures. Some have troubled the flesh for as many as and the step just beyond that impressive tally, in the case of Marilyn Monroe and perhaps a few others, already long before.

CHAPTER 11

Fashion and Style Icons

The landscape of fashion has been changing ever since the beginning of time. Styles come and go, with thousands of different combinations, melting pots of culture and modernity. In recent history, a handful of celebrities have proven to be timeless, turning into fashion icons. Their influence wields a heavy hand, their styles can spark fast trends, and several trends pop in and out of fashion each season. However, there are always some that don't end up quite fitting that mold, instead sticking out in the mind.

Today, we will delve a little more into the topic of fashion and style icons, people that captivate the hearts and minds of society through the neverending timeline of history. Their popularity does not drop, nor does their stylish influence. No matter what fashion trend takes over, these fashion and style icons retain their timeless charm.

Marilyn Monroe: a sex symbol that combined the sensuality of her poses with a touch of elegance, all in American wavy hair. This sexy red background photo shows the essence of a pivotal figure in the history of cinema. She has left an indelible signature in Hollywood and in the world. Her fashion icons are so engraved in the sands of time, they resurface every time someone seeks a costume for a party.

Audrey Hepburn: she was a famous British actress and fashion icon. She was an icon of fashion but especially of elegance and refinement. Women love to recall her famous simple and yet sophisticated little black dress. Also she wore gloves that went up to the elbow, combined with a large necklace with a charm. They are all distinctive fashion styles of the famous Audrey Hepburn, the combination of class and refinement.

Coco Chanel: in 1913, the French couturier Coco Chanel created her 'Maison de Haute Couture. Her elegance was the sentiment of the day. She is known for popularizing a sporty, casual chic as the feminine standard in the post-World War I era, and is often credited as the designer of the women's turn into more than trouser attire. At the time she introduced menswear to women, and created them out of jersey fabrics, which further popularized sportswear. She popularized a few common stylistic standards embodied by famous fashion and style icons, from tweed to the LBD. She is also famous for saying: "I take the money to the bank myself. Call my secretary if you have to paddle through banks of flowers or hoards of paparazzi."

Twiggy: British actress and singer who rose to fame in 1966, known not only for her singing and acting, but especially for being a national fashion trend as a leading model of the 60s. As a model she appeared over 500 times in British fashion magazines. She was one of the first teenagers of the '60s to join the singer model at the time. Her signature look, pixie cut, and stick-thin figures became emblems of the decade. Twiggy was thin and androgynous, which was different than the petite and hourglass standard favored by fashion houses, which was highly successful, making her the world's first supermodel with the signature look: blond pixie haircut and exaggerated long eyelashes. Twiggy helped to give model status more popularity because she was famous in the UK rather than just in the US. Twiggy set an example for those who think they could never become a model because they could become her supermodel. Twiggy has left such an influence in the beauty and fashion industry that people look back at her as an ageless beauty.

Trendsetters in Fashion

For better or worse, fashion rulemakers have always come and gone - inspired or horrified, we inherently follow along. This collection pays apt homage to the very best of them, celebrating a pearly paternity of pantheon gods. These are the gifted geniuses, the daring adventurers, those who have always had our interests at heart. For the most part, history's trendsetters in fashion share one thing in common: their blurred sexual fringe kept them forever wandering on the outside of mores and conventions. With the backbone bits of our current fashion breed stabilizing themselves beneath the glow of modernism's neon lights, the eternal has begun to stand farther and freer.

Our choice of 87 fashion-related icons here sheds a dim, luminous little spotlight at those gifted individuals whose creation of "outfitting" ideals impress us still. A look at the 17th to 20th century movers and shakers who have forever helped cast a sartorial vital thrall upon popular culture, surrounding us so thoroughly it's nearly invisible. This factor speaks not only to the functionality of the outline they provided (any one of the items these icons left behind can be said to have sunk in deep forever), but also to the power of their absolute address and stance in the realm of customization and effect. These daring darlings were vibrantly inventive as public personalities, nimble original artists producing the body that fits. Many set a course into the unwieldy territories that we now associate with sci-fi, punk, pop, and retro – and, in some secret lifeblood way, still define the twists and turns of the twenty-first-century zeitgeist. Their visions have outlived them, each remaining priceless museum artifact fiercely held in safe manufacture. Every one of the thirteen zed has left us, that is our legacy.

CHAPTER 12

Sports Icons

President John F. Kennedy famously observed that "victory has a hundred fathers and defeat is an orphan." That aphorism suggests that the iconic is ultimately triumphant, whether or not it should be. In athletic competition, however, sports fans recognize that victory is not always clear and that defeat often has many fathers, as well. Nevertheless, there is no denying that sport has produced such remarkable statues as Babe Ruth, Jack Dempsey, Jesse Owens, Joe Louis, Ted Williams, Sugar Ray Robinson, Mickey Mantle, Rocky Marciano, Wilt Chamberlain, Bill Russell, Muhammad Ali, Jim Brown, Willie Mays, Jackie Robinson, Arnold Palmer, Jim Thorpe, Hank Aaron, Roger Staubach, and "Shoeless" Joe Jackson, as well as global sports icons Pele and Diego Maradona.

Sports icons represent the American Dream and its fundamental ethos in a unique way. In the United States, athletes are, disproportionately, individuals who rose from rather modest or humble circumstances to a position of relative wealth, fame, and acclaim. In yet another way, though, sports icons are idols who run quite apart from the cultural norm in the United States, where people often harbor doubts, if not downright cynicism, about individuals and institutions of authority. Public figures in other endeavors, such as acting, politics, and business, rarely, if ever, attain iconic status. Politicians are usually mistrusted. Corporate "big shots" may be feared, but they are not usually loved. Age does not wither them. Fitness can. When it does, though, sports fans respond with nothing but sympathy, appreciation, and admiration for lives that have profoundly touched their own, achieving heights of performance that, quite literally, may be aspirationally unattainable.

Legends in Sports

In today's special insights, let us throw the spotlight on some real-life legends who have secured a rare place in the hearts of people with not just their skills but because of the outstanding aura they had around them. The legends of sports! The engrossing manner in which some extraordinary individuals on this planet can dominate a sport to such an astonishing extent makes them exceptional entities. One has to actually witness up close the aura they carry to truly realize the meaning of greatness. And it is the sheer weight of their enigma and our undying love for them that no matter how far away from the field of play they are today, we don't forget them, do we? After all, didn't someone say legends never die?

The sporting world has always had its share of epoch-making heroes; legendary musketeers who redefined the sport and took it to higher echelons with their mastery. Some of them may have been out for a relatively short time, but their aura still lingers in the minds of the people who watched them in action or inherited their talents. Then you have athletes who have had long and fulfilling careers, yet they continue to cast their everlasting shadows on the sportspersons of today. They do nothing, still do everything. The magnitude of their legacy is so overpowering that it relegates almost everything else happening in the modern era to mere afterthoughts. And that, everyone, is what we call a 'Legend'.

CHAPTER 13

Enduring Influence

These celebrities' influence and popularity is arguably greater now than it was during their lifetimes. This is in part because they died young and in the prime of their talent, but it is also because they have become eternal icons. From leading fans to make pilgrimages to their graves, preserving and celebrating their former homes, and immortalizing them in museums around the world, there is an enduring appeal. People used to say 'you can't be too rich or too thin' - today, it might be you can't be too dead and too famous. Unequivocally, being young, attractive, gifted and dead adds up to being hip. They continue to be commercial forces: numerous books, movies, records or merchandise about them have emerged in our own time.

Exploring the extraordinary afterlives of these 13 celebrities, this feature aims to elucidate why they still hold such allure for people, nearly a century and a half after cinema began. Individuals never "age" in memory in the way that buildings do and so can attract and maintain some lasting familiarity and hence affection. The resonance of the individual human story of talent, tragedy and loss - as well as the simple value of his or her creative work - is a draw. Some sites focus more on gaining an authentic sense of "being there" and "walking in the footsteps" of the figures who once lived in that place; others highlight a sustained engagement with music, film and pop culture. All celebrate the endearing, poignant markers of famous lives that endure across generations.

Legacy of Icons

In the world of toys, it pays to be an iconic figure. Whether that figure is a historical leader, an Emmy-Award winning musician, or straight-up royalty, if children and adults alike will build you a tribute from blocks, odds are you've left quite an impression. An iconic presence looms in popular culture—the pantheon of potential toy subjects. In this section, we focus on this enduring presence: the legacy of icons.

Icons are the sort of people that are remembered long after their time in the spotlight; they become a part of history, whether they were intended to or not. The Beatles, the Chief Justices of the United States, civil rights leaders and pop culture symbols—they might even have been. As a culture, we love a myth and remember a good myth-teller. Consider the reach that significant 20th-century icons had and continue to have and spread their personal influence. Albert Einstein has become one of the most revered scientists in the history of the world. He has impacted physics like no other individual: he laid the foundation of the modern theory of relativity, made significant contributions to quantum mechanics and never said women weren't good at science.

CHAPTER 14

Conclusion

It is the people below the surface who form the image, the inspiration, the encouragement, and the model for an icon-maker. Like a ring of ripples widening away from a stone thrown into a pond, their influence widens and fills the world far beyond the limits of their few years of physical life and becomes an expanding universe for the rest of us who continue to experience and internalize it. They walk most closely with us who ponder and meditate on their image and impulse, and often we feel a conspicuous and urgent need to hold on to them and make them ours in whatever way we can. Flowing from this experience, the ordeal or task of an icon is to encapsulate and step into, and stand as, that image and impression which is redolent of the ineffable qualities of the person being given to matter. An icon offers the opportunity to enter the world or environment of thought and enthusiasm that has such talismanic power for those who love the individual behind the artistic presentation and it offers the perpetuity of material presence and mortal apprehension that a photograph does not.

Centraits remain animated wellsprings. They become companions, as writer my friend Tim Kashani calls them, opening the door and inviting us in to the quirks and curves, the setbacks and stumbles, and the marvels and landmark strides of their lives. Eternally immortalized, they permit us to experience vicariously the very forces that inform their unparalleled scope of wisdom and valor, grace and charm, resolve and sapience. Icons — in life, in death, and for centuries after their spirits are called back to the core of creation — remain electrified with the essence of a life well-lived. Their brilliance brings out the beauty and courage in all of us. Their luminosity is to be treasured, preserved, and honored. They are a call to our mirror in stone to reflect the candor of their incarnations and to stand as truthful witnesses to the foibles and heights of humanity — them and in our own time in the ethereal journey that is recorded in earth minerals. Through their icons' artifices, eternal inspiration is delivered to us. That is the magic of our icons: they are more than just people. They are the person divine, their essence forever enshrined.

Reflecting on the Lives of Eternal Icons

For millennia, society has celebrated the lives of beloved and revered figureheads and icons. Warriors, kings, and leaders have been raised to the status of demigods, one way or another, through tales and legends. Undefined by time, they have become part of the world's narrative. They are much lauded through poetry, plays, operas, paintings, and film, and are preserved through shared memory, cultural art, and written word.

Today, within this book, we reflect on the modern-day synonyms for those demigods of yore. These are celebrities; those actors, politicians, sportspeople, and philosophers whom we deem, either unanimously or through a shared respect, worthy to become a part of our world narrative. These passionate testimonials and reflections are a small but important consolation through their shared grief. Given the legacy of these celebrities and under their inspiration, we explore what makes life meaningful and the choices we make worth the while.

For the most part, if and when a celebrity passes, it captures the world's attention. We are captivated by their lives, by the complex lives and loves, and often equally as complex, their abuse, fragility, torment, and suffering, at the dangerous delight of our voyeur's gaze. They roar, scream, laugh, and cry, bellow and pierce the delicate, multi-pitched music that is the human condition. In their absence, they are dearly missed.

There are hallowed, hagiographic representations of our lionized heroes in the sports stadium, the stage, on one's cinema screen, or pictorially, framed in our living rooms, creating a shrine of the heart. When such exuberant, often charismatic, and powerfully driven people leave us, an entropic sort of chill penetrates the air, reverberating in a roar of grief. Their death, in a twist of irony and testament, offers a profound sense of gratitude and humbled reflection of their life. These impassioned dedications symbolize a collective appreciation for lives that have left a shared, enduring legacy, echoing the words of George Eliot, in the last of her novels, Daniel Deronda, that, in essence, states that in the life we lead, even in our absence, we are a part of the universal story. Our lives echo everlasting in the silent, eventual awe of imperishable memory.